# How to Grow Tomatoes!

From

How To Mastery

# Contents

# Disclaimer

Look these things have to be here so let's just get this out of the way and then we can get started. This book contains information designed and intended to show people how to grow the healthiest and best tomato plants possible. It is intended for educational purposes only and there is no guarantee that you will produce monster sized tomatoes or be able to feed and entire country from the yield of your plants. Everyone's garden is different and there are a lot of factors involved in the growth and fruit production of plants. Plus, there is the issue of the human element and the amount of effort used. Lastly, there is the issue of using good old common sense. The information in this book, either all or some of it, might not work in your particular situation. It is the responsibility of the reader to decide which information is relevant and makes sense for their own garden. The writers, publishers, and distributors of this book assume no responsibility for any or all of the information in this book. Now that this is out of the way, let's get started!

# Introduction

Tomatoes are among the most popular plants when it comes to home gardens. Even people without a home garden grow tomatoes in a planter or other container. Why? Because nothing beats the taste of a fresh homegrown tomato on a sandwich or burger. Nothing beats the crispness of a fresh tomato on a salad either.

Tomatoes are also fairly easy to grow as well if you know how. But there is a different between growing tomatoes and GROWING tomatoes! I have a lot of success with my tomato crop. Every year I have many more tomatoes than I can handle and I wind up reducing the number of plants but still have a lot to give away to friends, neighbors, ever demanding relatives and co-workers.

People who see my plants are amazed at the size and yield of the tomato plants in it. My plants routinely grow to over 6 feet tall and the yield is amazing. One year I picked over 3,500 cherry tomatoes from just 5 plants!

Plus, my beefsteak tomatoes easily cover an entire bun on my burgers! The plants get so high and so loaded with fruit that they sometimes break the wooden poles I use to support the plants!

In this book I will share some of the things I do to have such great success with my tomato plants and the other plants in my garden. There is no super secret magic fertilizer or special compounds that you need to buy from me or any of that nonsense. Everything I will show you can be easily accomplished by any home gardener using materials and products available at just about every home and garden center.

Let's also take a moment to dispel another fear some of you might have as well. The methods I use are designed to SAVE work not create it. If you knew me you would know that I do not believe in working hard when you don't have to. I believe in getting results and doing the things needed to get those results. But I'm all for making everything as simple and easy as possible.

I will say that everyone's results will vary according to their own location and the things they do when they set up and maintain their garden. You may do better than me but you might do worse than me as well. It's all in where you are and what you do. But I guarantee you that if you follow the advice and procedures outlined in this book you will increase your yield and have healthier plants.

Last but certainly not least, sometimes you will see information repeated through this book. Some things might be repeated a few times. I do this not for filler or for making the book appear longer and better than it is but rather because sometimes information pertains to more than one topic.

Since some people do not read a book like this from start to finish, I found out through experience that it is best to provide all the information needed to understand a particular topic at the same time I discuss that topic. This is because some people go right for a particular chapter and want to learn about a specific item first even though it might be at the end of the book. By repeating things when necessary, everyone gets the very best chance of learning what they need when they need it.

In other words, the content in this book has been laid out and written in such a manner to produce the very best results possible. People who read our books learn more with less confusion when we use this approach. Since we have been writing these books for over 25 years, we figure we know how to do it right!

So let's get started shining up the old green thumb and start learning how we can grow bigger and better tomatoes in our home garden!

# Varieties of Tomatoes

Just like there is more than one type and model of car for you to choose from, there are several different types of tomatoes that you can grow in your garden. You can choose from size and shape, taste and yield. There are the standard types of tomatoes that people have grown for hundreds of years and new genetic hybrids that were created to be more disease resistant and produce different types of fruit.

Though it is not practical to list every single type of tomato available in every part of the world, here are some of the most common types and a short description of each one to get you started. For more choices and what is recommended in your area, I would suggest visiting your local garden center or getting a copy of one of the popular seed catalogs which will give you more choices and more information.

For the most part, tomatoes are referred to by their 3 basic types of applications. We have **slicing tomatoes** which are your larger sized tomatoes usually used on sandwiches and burgers and in salads. Slicing tomatoes tend to be juicier and have thinner outer walls and larger gel chambers inside.

Then we have **cherry tomatoes** which are your very small tomatoes, usually the size of a golf ball or smaller. These plants produce a LOT of tomatoes and are great for snacking, salads and other applications.

Finally we have paste tomatoes which are primarily used for making tomato sauce and tomato paste. These tomatoes are less juicer than slicers and have thicker outer walls. The insides are firmer than slicers as well.

For now, though, here are the basic names of tomato plants:

**Beefsteak** – This is a slicer and a large tomato. There are hybrids of the beefsteak that can grow to several pounds and completely cover a burger in one slice! Varieties include Big Boy, Better Boy, and Supersonic.

**Celebrity** – This is a medium sized tomato and is good for all around use. A slicer, it is tasty and juicy and will lend itself to almost any application. Some refer to these types of tomatoes as "globe" tomatoes because of their very round shape.

**Sweet 100** – This is a cherry tomato and the design of this plant was made to produce a very high yield. Each grouping of tomatoes on the plant can be up to 12 or more tomatoes! Each plant can produce several hundred of these small beauties in one season!

**Yellow Pear** – This is a yellow tomato that grows in the shape of a pear.

**Roma** – This tomato grows in the shape of a plum and is referred to as a plum tomato for that very reason.

**Early Girl** – This is a slicing tomato designed to mature early, usually in 45-60 days. This is a good choice for areas where you have a shorter than normal growing season.

**Better Bush** – These hybrid plants will grow in smaller containers and are referred to as dwarf plants. They will produce smaller fruit but the small size of the plant allows it to be grown in containers on patios and such. May also be named "small fry" for obvious reasons.

**Heat Master** – This hybrid is designed to grow well in very hot climates where other tomatoes might not fare so well.

**Lemon Boy** – Medium sized yellow tomato with a medium growing season.

**Brandywine** – One of the most popular slicing tomatoes with fruits in the 1.5 pound range. Very tasty as well and a favorite for a lot of people.

**San Marzano** – this is a paste tomato known for producing great flavor for all types of sauces and pastes.

**Sungold** – these are very sweet orange tomatoes.

**Cherokee Green** – These green tomatoes are easy to grow and tasty. Not usually found at garden centers, though.

**Micro Tom** – This hybrid can actually be grown indoors if you have the sunlight and room!


These are just some of the approx. 7500 varieties of tomatoes that are in existence today. There is something for everyone when it comes to tomato plants. Be sure to check out the type and size of the fruit as well as the suitability for your particular region.

Ask your local agriculture department or garden center what type of diseases are commonplace in your region as well. If there are any diseases that you should be concerned with, try and find a hybrid plant that is designed to be resistant to that disease.

And of course, you can search online for the plants you want based on area and disease resistance. Gardening is a lot of trial and error in the beginning. There are so many different tomatoes and some have their own distinctive tastes and texture. What one person might love another person might hate so reviews will get you only so far.

I suggest that in the first year or two you plant several different varieties to see which ones you like. Then, as you find out your favorites, grow more of those the next year. Don't be afraid to try something new!

# Garden Layout

Sometimes the most important things happen during the planning stages and growing tomatoes are no exception. Tomatoes like a lot of sun so it is important that we pick a spot that has sun a good portion of the day. That means several factors need to be considered before any plant goes in the ground.

**Exposure**

The tomato plants love sun so the exposure can be a critical thing to consider. Note the position of the sun in the sky during the growing season not in the winter. The sun will usually be higher in the sky during the summer depending on where you live.

Make sure the sun will not be blocked out by surrounding structures or by trees and shrubs. Try and make this determination when the trees have leaves on them. Do not look at your proposed plot during the winter and see sun and figure it's going to be perfect. Note where the sun comes from. If it is shining through the branches, that's not good because leaves will block at least some of the sun in the summer months.

Some sites might be fine this year and next but keep in mind that trees grow taller over time so pick a spot where tress are not likely to cover with shade for at least the next few years. That will at least cut down on some of the work involved in preparing a brand new site later on.

**Soil Type**

While we will get into soil I far more detail later, for now let's just say the area in which you plant your garden should have a decent quality soil. If it is full or rocks and root and boulders and other kind of crap, it is best to look somewhere else. If the soil in a location is full or sand or hard as a rock, you might wish to look elsewhere as well. But as we said, more details on soil later.

**Other Plants**

Think about what kind of plants you are going to have in your garden. If you are just growing tomatoes, then you are fine if you just have one row of plants. But if you are growing other plants, or more than one row of tomatoes, then you have to figure out the best placement for your plants. This is VERY important.

As we said in the introduction, tomato plants can grow to over 6 feet tall under the right conditions.

That means that plants in back of your tomatoes (in relation to the position of the sun) will be shaded by the tomatoes as they grow. So keep your tomato plants in the rear parts of the garden so they can get sunlight as well as the shorter plants.

That means that ground plants like lettuce and carrots should be in the front of the garden where they will get more sun. Then plants like peppers will follow and taller plants like our tomatoes will be behind the peppers.

If you have multiple rows of tomatoes, then stagger plant them so each plant will receive more sun. For example, plant the first row of plants starting at the end of the row and space the plants 3 feet apart. Start the next row 18" from the end and plant every 3 feet as well. The result is that you can see each plant from the front of the garden and each plant will get more sun. No plant will be exactly behind another plant.

This might seem like a little thing but it can make a big difference when it comes to plant growth and yield. Every little thing helps.

## Accessibility

Think about how easy it is going to be working on your garden, watering it and carrying the produce back to the house during harvesting.

We want to have a convenient spot so that it is as easy as possible to do everything we need to do during the gardening season.

If you pick a spot that is 300 feet from the nearest water faucet, you are not as likely to drag out 300 feet of hose to water the garden every day as you would if the hose was right there a few feet away. It's just human nature to want to avoid things that are a lot of work so let's try and make everything as easy as possible!

In fact, the availability of water is one of the most important factors when considering where you garden should be located. The closer to an outdoor faucet the better. If you are going to build a dedicated automatic watering system like we will be showing you later, you are not going to want garden hose lying all across your lawn for the entire summer!

**Size of Garden**

Know how much room you can dedicate to your garden. You want to have enough room to grow the things you want without crowding your plants. Plants need air and space to grow healthy root systems. So have a good idea what plants you want to grow and how many of each type you want as well.

Look on the plant label or seed package to get the recommended spacing requirements and then FOLLOW those requirements. If you have to make a judgment call then always go with more space between plants and fewer plants. Crowding plants reduces yield, decreases plant health and makes it easier for disease and insects to spread from one plant to another.

One thing a lot of new gardeners, and more than a few old timers forget is to allow access for the gardener to get around the plants to weed, apply any insecticides or other chemicals and of course to harvest the fruit from the plants. There has been more than a few times when I lost a nice 2 pound tomato because I couldn't see the damned thing because of access issues!

You should be able to look around the entire plant so you can inspect for insect damage and other problems. Miss a tomato cutworm today and half the plant will be gone tomorrow!

## Appearance/Aesthetics

Part of the enjoyment of gardening is keeping the peace at home. Sometimes one spouse or another might have an aversion to seeing the garden all day long. They may prefer to have it on the side of the yard where it is blocked from everyday view.

Some people, though, like the look of a garden and enjoy looking at it while sitting on the deck or the patio. So just keep in mind the wishes of everyone when it comes time to decide on your garden site.

One advantage of having an inside view of the garden is that you will notice certain situations faster such as an animal eating your plants or a fallen plant or something like that. It's a small consideration we grant you, but still something to consider.

## Your Ability

While you might want to hear this, sometimes gardens can get to be a bit too much for some of us as we get older. Design a garden that is well within your limits and abilities. Remember that gardening is supposed to be enjoyable not a huge chore that overwhelms you during the hot months or summer.

Your garden should be large enough to fit your needs but small enough for you to maintain and weed in the cool morning or evening hours. Don't give yourself more than you can handle by planting too large a garden.

# Soil Type & Preparation

Most people are aware of two purposes soil has for our plants. That is to provide moisture and to carry nutrients to the plant as well. But most people don't think of two other important things soil does for our plants. Soil also allows our plants to develop nice deep and strong root systems and also helps stabilize the plant during winds and rain.

## Soil Type

To say that the type and consistency of soil is important would still be an understatement. The fact is, the type and quality of the soil is the single most important aspect of your garden. You can buy the best plants, maintain the garden to the best of your ability and use the best fertilizer but if the soil is crap, you'll have a crappy garden as well. (By the way, "crap" is an official gardening term! At least in this book!)

One of the most important aspects of the soil when it comes to tomatoes and most other vegetables is that it should be fairly loose in consistency. This will allow the root system to spread down further and become stronger and less sensitive to variations in soil moisture. The deeper the roots are allowed to penetrate, the better it is for the overall health of the plant.

Mostly solid soil like clay will prohibit deep rooting and result in more roots spread across the upper regions of the soil. This provides very little protection against draught and also gives little in the way of strength for the plant. We want the roots to grow as full and as deep as possible which means getting as little resistance from the soil as possible as well.

**Tilling or Loosening the Soil**

Most oil on new garden areas will be compacted from years of walking mowing, rain and overall settling. Therefore, before a garden can be planted, this compacted soil must be loosened up. This can be done manually with a shovel and a rake or with a power tilling machine.

Make no mistake this is hard work and will take some muscle and some time to complete.

I strongly advise that you use a tiller or sub contract this part of the work whenever possible. Quite frankly there is nothing pleasurable about turning over soil. Buy or rent a tiller or sub contract it out.

The soil should be turned over to a depth of at least 8 inches. This will bring most of the rocks and roots to the surface so that they can be removed. Rocks and debris can interfere with the growth of the plants and rocks can break a tiller machine if they get jammed in the blades. So as you uncover a large rock, toss it aside so it will be out of your way.

It has been my experience that if you are tilling over the soil you should do so in two directions. One pass up and down and a second pass right to left. Sort of like a checkerboard pattern when you get through. This will insure that no parts get missed and that the soil is thoroughly broken up.

The soil should be very loose almost like sand when you are done. If there are still clumps and hard parts after you are done, make another pass or two. This should take only a few minutes and the results will be well worth it.

Breaking up and tilling the soil also adds air into the soil as well as mix up the material that may be on the surface and bring it down into the soil. Tilling in mulch or other matter into the soil will enrich the soil, aid in decomposition and feed your plants better.

In fact, tilling at the beginning of every season helps bring that old mulch down into the soil and allows it to replenish much of what was removed by the plants last year. Mulch also helps the soil say loose and absorbent.

## Soil PH

Tomatoes are acidic creatures and they do very well when the soil is somewhat acidic in nature. Tomatoes like soil that has a PH of approx 6.0 – 6.8. Since neutral PH is about 7.0. 6.0 is slightly acidic.

How do you check the PH of your soil? There are two ways. First, you can take a soil sample to your local garden center or agriculture office. For a fee they will test your soil for PH and other items that they feel are relevant. If this is not practical for you, there are home PH testers available for less than $30 and you can use them year after year.

How often should you test your soil? Well, it's kind of like how often should you go to the doctor? You go every year for a physical and then whenever you develop a problem or need. So we should test our soil at the beginning and end of each gardening season as well as whenever any or all of our plants don't seem to be doing well or show signs of stress.

Since testing is so easy with a home PH tester, I recommend testing once or twice during the season as well. Test a few different locations in case there are any differences in the soil. Add lime or other additives to get your soil back to where it needs to be. Your local garden center can assist you with the proper Additives for your own situation.

**Fertilizers**

Personally I am not a fan of adding fertilizer to the soil prior to planting. Though others might disagree with this approach, I find that adding fertilizer into the soil before planting can cause the fertilizer to come into direct contact with the roots of the plants and this can burn them.

What I usually do is use mulch to feed the plants and soil and supplement that with a general purpose liquid fertilizer that is sprayed on with a sprayer or garden hose. In my opinion, this is a much safer way of feeding seedling and other newly planted plants.

Spraying fertilizer such as Miracle-Gro or other liquid fertilizer actually helps feed the plant in two ways. First and foremost, the liquid seeps down in the soil and then gets drawn into the roots along with other moisture. This feeds the nutrients to the plant in the conventional way.

But some of the liquid fertilizer will sit on the leave and be absorbed through the plant surface as well. Exactly how much I am not sure of but any time we can provide the plant with more of what it needs, and be able to do it in a safe manner, that is good.

Just be sure to mix and apply any chemical according to the manufactures instructions. Do not apply a heavier or more concentrated dose thinking it will work better. It might burn the roots or kill the plant.

For those of us liking the all natural method of growing tomatoes, instead of using fertilizer, add mulch to the soil and till it under to mix it with the soil. This will decompose and produce nutrition for the plant without chemicals. Use the approach that appeals to you and don't concern yourself with what other people feel is best. Natural fertilizing is an accepted method of gardening.

If you are adding mulch into your new garden bed, give it a week or so and retest the PH to make sure that whatever was added to the soil did not dramatically alter the soil PH levels. Adjust the PH as necessary to get to the 6.0-6.8 level.

**Moisture Retention**

As we already stated, one of the most important things that soil does is deliver moisture to the roots of the plant.

While this is not a problem when there is constant moisture, it can cause a problem if the soil is very sandy and is not capable of holding water in suspension in the soil between watering.

Sandy soil allows the water to percolate down more quickly than clay or loam type of soils. If you soil is very sandy and allows water to pass through too easily, it will quickly dry out and stress the plant. Since this is bad for the plant we need to find a way of increasing the moisture holding ability of the soil.

The easiest way of doing this is to add something like a loam soil or peat moss to the soil by tilling it in the soil. The loam or peat has a higher ability to hold water and this will help improve that aspect of the soil in your garden. Another alternative would be to add amounts of mulch to the soil and over time this should increase water retention as well. Peat moss will act faster so you might want to add some peat moss and some mulch and allow the two materials to work together.

Tomato plants require a LOT of moisture to produce a high yield. But too much water is not good either. If you routinely notice puddles or standing water shortly after watering then perhaps your soil is holding too much water and not allowing it to drain properly. This can lead to plant and root rot and an increased chance of diseases to the plant.

Plus, standing water is a wonderful breeding ground for insects and insects and plants are not good companions when it comes to producing a good yield of health fruit.

**Soil Preparation**

We have already given you most of the basics for prepping your soil but here it is in a step by step format to make it easier for you:

Starting about a month before planting, break up soil using a shovel or tiller. Make several passes until soil has no large clumps. Soil should be tilled down to about 8 inches.

Remove rocks, roots and other debris. The result should be a nice and loose soil with no foreign matter in it.

Rake soil smooth and remove any additional surface debris.

Check soil water retention and add sand or peat moss as needed to either reduce or increase water holding ability.

Prior to planting, check PH again to make sure mulch or anything else has not changed it.

Add mulch to top of soil to start decomposition process and to help keep moisture in the upper levels of the soil.

I cannot stress to you enough about how critical soil type and consistency is to growing tomatoes. Shallow roots and stressed plants can easily occur in soil that does not allow the proper root structure to form.

For a plant to be and remain healthy requires nutrition and moisture. Take every opportunity now to provide as high a quality soil to your new plants. It is far easier to do this now than after plants are in the soil. A few more minutes now can mean all the difference in your harvest and yield.

# Plants vs. Seeds

Let me start right off the bat telling you that most of the decision concerning starting plants from seed or buying seedlings is strictly personal preference. There is nothing wrong with buying seedlings and nothing wrong with starting your own plants from seed. So don't get offended or dismiss any information written about either method. Just read it because you might get some insight into something!

I have tried starting tomatoes from seeds for many years. I've had some success and some failure. What I can say is that starting plants from seeds takes some time, some patience, and some dedicated room in a heated space inside your home near a window.

If you are planting seeds then you need to give yourself some time to get the seeds started early enough so they can be seedlings when planting time comes. This can be anywhere from 6-8 weeks depending on the type of plant and where you live.

One thing I do not skimp on is seeds. I buy name brand seeds and I make sure they are dated for this growing season. You can use last year's seeds but the germination rate will be less so you should plant more in order to get the number you have in mind. But really, seeds are so cheap you really shouldn't have to use last years left overs. Splurge and get some fresh seeds.

Start the plants in peat pots or peat containers filled with a high quality potting soil. Place a few seeds in each pot. You can thin some out later if every seed germinates. Keep the soil heated to roughly 75 degrees and make sure you keep the plants and soil moist at all times. Allowing the pot or soil to dry out even once can kill the new plant. Moisture at this stage is critical.

As the plants sprout and grow, continue adding water to keep the soil moist. Don't make it too wet or you will rot the plant. Just keep the soil moist. As plants get taller, remove the scrawny or weaker plants until you have one strong plant per pot or pod. After plants get taller you can reduce to soil tem to between 60 and 70 degrees.

Before planting outside, it is important that you allow your plants to "get used" to being outside. This is called "hardening" the plants. For a few days, place your plants outdoors a little bit each day gradually increasing the time they remain outside.

Bring them in if it starts raining or if the temperatures get too cold. Hardening the plant will help it survive its first few weeks outside more easily.

If all this seems like a lot of work, it can be. Starting plants from seeds requires attention and work. But for some people the rewards that come from seeing your own creations grow makes it all worthwhile. For others this is not a big deal. So whatever group you are in, just do what feels best for you.

Personally, I always found that the plants at my local garden center just looked healthier. The size of the plants was larger and the branches and trunks were larger in diameter. Instead of tall and gangly seedlings, these plants looked like miniature versions of full sized plants. They just looked better. I've planted both and just did not notice much of a difference in yield between the two either.

I also buy from an established garden center because I know where the plants came from. This cannot be said buying them off the side of the road or from your local supermarket. Generally speaking, the more untrained or uncaring hands that touch your plant, the more chances that the plants might have been stressed at some point before you bought them. Again, this is just for my peace of mind and I have no factual data on this whatsoever. What can I say, it's just me.

So after several years of growing my own plants, I now use plants from the garden center. I make one trip, pick out the healthiest plants in the store, and go home and plant them. The plants are usually already hardened because they were outside in the garden center and I have yet to have any kind of transplant problem either.

Naturally it is more expensive to buy plants than it is to grow from seed but the cost is still fairly low. You can get plants from as low as $1.50 all the way up to larger plants for $10. I always buy the smaller plants and usually have no problem getting them to grow and catch up to their larger brothers at the store. But that's just me and you should do whatever you feel most comfortable with.

Generally speaking the larger the plant you buy the faster it will produce fruit after it is planted because it is further along in the growth process. But even with the cheapest small plants I always get a good yield. Do whatever your budget and feelings tell you are best.

Always remember the quality of the plant you start with will have a large effect on your final harvest and yield. In other words, whether you plant from seed or buy plants, don't skimp here. Get or grow the best plants you can.

# Planting Your Tomatoes

Assuming you already have prepared your garden soil and picked the right location for your tomato plants, planting those plants is downright easy. After all, the soil is nice and loose and all you have to do is plop them in the ground and move on, right? Well. Almost.

Your plants or seedlings should be planted outdoors after all chances of frost are gone. Frost will quickly kill a seedling or new young plant so we must be careful. I like to give it an extra week or two after frost is likely just in case we have a cold snap or two. The exact time of year will vary depending on where you live. Your local agriculture department or garden center can let you know when it is safe to plant your plants outdoors.

Make sure your soil is as free of weeds as possible. Remember that weeds take nutrients and moisture from the soil that should be going to your garden plants, not the weeds. It is easier to weed at this time. When you are done weeding, rake the soil smooth and you are ready to plant.

If there is mulch already on the top of the soil, move it aside and create a hole where you wish to plant your new plant. Make sure the mulch stays a few inches away from the stem of the plant to enable it to harden off and not get burned from the mulch. Eventually this will not matter but when a plant is very young, this is a good idea.

If there are roots coming of out the pot or starter pod, gently pull them slightly away from the pod or pot so the soil will go all around them when they are inserted in the planting hole. While it is not critical that this is done, it takes only a few seconds and can make it easier for the roots to grow into the soil and start feeding the plants.

Your plant should be buried in the ground up to the main stalk that comes out of the pot. Some people say to plant it up to the first leaves because eventually the plant will grow roots all along the parts of the plant that are beneath the ground. But at least plant it so that the soil in the garden completely covers the pod or pot the plant was planted in. If the soil is loose enough to enable the plant to go deeper then do it.

Another alternative is to plant your tomato plant lying down in a trough dug down deep enough to cover the pod or pot. Then lay the plant in the trough and gently bend the end of the plant so it is sticking up and cover the rest of the plant with soil.

This is another way of getting more of the stem underground without digging deep into the soil.

You can apply fertilizer into the hole that you dig but always remember that we must be very careful to avoid burning the roots of the plants. There are special fertilizers for this application. They are called seed bed fertilizers and you can get them online or in your garden center. Do NOT use powdered fertilizers directly in the planting hole as these will likely burn the roots unless they are specifically designated for this purpose.

Follow the manufacturer's directions carefully and do not use a higher concentration. Personally, I tend to mix a slightly weaker mixture just to be on the safe side a little bit. Remember you can always add fertilizer later if you wish after the plant has been transplanted. Fertilizer applied after planting with be somewhat weakened by passage through the soil so danger of burning the roots is reduced. But is you apply too much of anything to the soil or the plant problems can arise.

The mixing of any kind of chemical is definitely NOT one of those "more is better" situations. Always mix and apply according to the instructions.

Doing anything else can place the health of the plant, as well as your own health and the health of your family at risk!

I also suggest that you plant your plants in neat rows with some kind of organization. First of all it just looks nicer and better. Secondly, it makes identifying plants versus weeds easier. Sometimes weeds can come very close to looking like vegetable plants and you can get confused.

The last reason for planting in neat rows is that it makes weeding and soil cultivation a lot easier. You can just go straight down a row with whatever tools you might be using and it just makes things a lot easier.

While we will discuss watering a little later in far more detail, let's just say for now watering is extremely important. Water your newly planted plants after you plant them. This will help compact the loose soil around them and transfer water to the roots to help them get established. You don't have to water them heavily, just enough to get them started.

The upper parts of the soil MUST stay moist or damp all the time. This is where the plants will draw their moisture and nutrients from until the plants develop a stronger and deeper root structure. So make an extra effort to make sure the ground stays moist for the first several weeks at least.

I also like to place some kind of sign indicating what type of plant it is. Most all tomato plants look very similar and you might have planted several different types. I always have a drawing of what is planted where but having a stake or sick with a sign on it is very helpful as well.

# Watering

After you have planted your garden, the plants need 3 things to survive and produce a harvest. The first thing is sunlight and hopefully you have nicely provided for that with a perfect spot that lets the sun shine down on your plants all day long.

The second thing is nutrients which hopefully will come from the soil, mulch and possibly other things. We will talk about that a little more in a while. In fact, though it is not recommended, if you provide sunlight and water, your plants might do perfectly fine without any additional food. At least for this year maybe.

But the one thing your plants will not be able to survive without is water. Water is needed for the processes within the plant to keep going and help the plant grow and stay alive. Without water, the plant will go into shock and eventually die. While most people understand this, there is a significant amount of misunderstandings concerning watering your garden. We will try and dispel some of those misconceptions when it comes to watering your garden.

## Misconception #1: More Water is Always Better

Though plants need enough water to satisfy their needs, too much water is not good for them either. Flooded soil is unstable and the excess moisture will subject the roots to root rot and other diseases.

It is not so much the quantity of water that is important but rather the ability of the soil to process the water and let it drain through the soil when it is not absorbed by the plant. There will be times when it will rain a lot during the day or it might rain for a few days straight. Good drainage soil will allow the moisture to percolate downward and not accumulate around the roots. Though there are some limits to the amount of time plants can be subjected to constant rain or watering, good drainage usually makes this a non-critical issue most of the time.

Limit your watering to when it is necessary and keep the duration long enough to make the ground moist down several inches while not making the soil loose or muddy. After a few weeks in your first garden you will have a pretty good idea of when you should water and for how long.

The outside temperature and the overall humidity and amount of sunlight will affect the amount of watering needed. A cool and cloudy day might not require much water at all while a hot and sunny day may require watering more than once.

You will notice wilting leaves when a tomato plant is suffering from not enough water. The leaves will be soft and hanging down and you cannot miss the sickly appearance. Applying water will allow the leaves to come back to normal very quickly. It is surprising how fast the leaves spring back.

But do not think it is all right to let the plant get to that point because the leaves come back to normal. The plant has still been stressed and this has an adverse effect on overall plant health. Try to avoid this type of condition by providing adequate water to all plants.

Too much water on the other hand can cause disease and root rot. In many cases the signs of distress may occur too late for any action to save the plant to be effective. To avoid this water only as long as needed and do not overwater. There usually is a considerable difference between normal watering and over watering. For example, if your garden needs 15 minutes worth or watering and you give it 30 minutes, nothing will probably happen. But if you give it 2 hours worth of watering, you are asking for trouble!

### Misconception #2: It Makes No difference when you Water

Some people have their own thoughts and ideas when it comes to the optimum time to water your garden.

For some it is just personal preference but there are some things you should be aware of when it comes to time of day and watering.

First of all, watering at night or in the evening is almost universally accepted to be a bad idea. This provides an ideal environment for disease and fungus because the sun never gets a chance to dry off the plants and the top of the soil or mulch. Because it is cooler and there is no sunlight, things stay wet or damp all night long.

Watering during the heat of the day or during high overhead sunlight is not a good idea for two reasons. First, the heat of the air and the temperature of the plants and soil may tend to evaporate some or most of the water before it even hits the ground. So much of the water is wasted.

Second, watering leaves droplets of water on the leaves of the plants. These droplets can act like little magnifying glasses and concentrate the sun's rays on the leaves burning them. This can damage or even kill the plant. When you take both of these conditions in mind, we can all agree that watering in the hot times of the day is not a good idea.

Of course, if you have not watered and your plants are showing signs of distress, you need to water immediately to get the moisture to the plants to avoid more damage. In those cases the rewards greatly outweigh the risks.

If you have to do this, direct most of the water to the soil and not to the plant itself to minimize the water burning issue. Placing a hose directly on the ground and allowing water to trickle in might be a good idea.

**Misconception #3: Deep Watering Every other Day is Better than Frequent Watering**

If there were one universal watering schedule for every garden, things would be much easier but unfortunately, that is not the case.

Once plants are established and have deeper root systems you might be able to get by with deep watering at less frequent times. But seedlings and new plants need constant moisture from the upper parts of the soil. They do not get moisture from deeper in the soil because they don't have roots there yet.

One practice you should not use is watering for short period of time several times a day. This might keep the upper parts of the sol damp but under that the soil will never get moisture. Since roots travel to where the moisture is in the soil, the result will be very shallow rooted plants which will produce a lot less fruit.

For this reason, water seedlings and new plants frequently but long enough so that the water will penetrate down further in the soil. This will encourage deeper root growth and will enable the plants to be more tolerant of upper soil moisture variations.

**Misconception #4: Watering Should be Done Manually**

While plants are smart and take the things they need from the air and the soil, they are not so smart that they can tell. Or even care, whether the water they receive comes from rain, a hose or a sprinkler. And the definitely do not care if the water is delivered by a person or via a timer.

Garden purists might tell you that watering by hand is the most accurate way to water because it allows you to see the soil and make adjustments to the water you deliver. They would be 100% right in those observations as well. But they omit other equally important factors as well.

Watering my hand is an exact process and no person will water the same way twice. Some plants will get more water than others some days and some plants might get too much while others get too little. It is because people are just not as accurate as a permanent watering system attached to a timer.

If the system is properly designed (We'll show you how at the end of this book) and the timer set for the average watering needed, you can automate your watering pretty darned successfully. You can go away on vacation and not have to depend on rainfall or a neighbor to water your garden. It's set it and forget it gardening.

If you enjoy watering and think you can do a great job then it's perfectly fine to go that way if that's what you want. But if you like the idea of things being done for you automatically while you do other things, there is nothing wrong with that either.

One of the great things about gardening is that it is a uniquely individual hobby. You grow what you want, where you want and how you want. In other words, if it works for you, go for it. Watering included.

## Watering Tip # 1: Use Mulch on the soil

Applying mulch on the soil helps keep the soil temperature more stable and will also cut down on the amount of water needed by a more than significant amount.

Sun beating down on the ground heats up the soil and also the moisture in it. The sun bakes the top area of the soil and dries it out very quickly. As we all know, many plants get their moisture from this upper part of the soil. If that area dries out, then the plant doesn't get the moisture it needs.

Seedlings, plants started from seeds, and shallow rooted plants are the most susceptible to damage from this kind of situation. Once your tomato plants get more established and grow deeper roots, they will become more and more immune to surface dryness. But until that time, keep the top of the soil moist.

Mulch can help that by shielding the soil from the direct rays of the sun and from air constantly moving over the soil. Mulch will insulate the soil and help it retain more moisture for longer periods of time. Therefore, less water is needed and watering does not have to be done as often as with uncovered soil.

Temperature is another important factor that mulch helps control. Mulch acts like an insulator and helps soil not get as hot during the day but also keeps it warmer at night because it traps some of the heat inside the soil and does not allow it to escape. This can help young plants and seedlings survive lower temps at night and help other plants survive longer at the end of the season.

Last but not least, mulch helps protect the plants by keeping a much more consistent soil temperature. There are fewer swings in temperature and this is good for overall plant health. In fact, the decomposition of the products in the mulch produces heat which provides a better environment for plant and root growth.

So make it your plan to add mulch to the top of the soil throughout the season. By the end of your season several inches of mulch will help your plants survive longer, stay healthier and use a heck of a lot less water.

## Watering Tip #2: Water Similar to the Way Nature Waters

First of all, most of what I am saying here is strictly personal preference. I'm not sure that there is any research or studies to confirm or dispute this but it works for me and it makes sense to me.

What I am talking about is that I like to water my garden in such a way that it is as close to rainfall as possible. That means watering from overhead where the water falls down on the plants and soil. Watering in this way might be an inefficient manner or watering because you will have some evaporation but I believe that staying as close to nature is always the right way to go.

I also believe that some moisture is absorbed through the leaves and branches of the plants as well. So watering from above not only gets water to the roots of the plant but also to the leaves and branches as well.

Does this really make much of a difference? As I have already said, I'm not sure but I have had a ton of success with all my plants with this kind of watering regimen. I am not someone who puts great faith in reports or studies. If it works for me, I'm going to keep on doing it. If it doesn't work, I'm moving on.

As with everything else when it comes to gardening, you make your own decision and do whatever is comfortable for you.

## Watering Tip #3: Automate Your Watering!

I do not like to be a slave to my garden. It is always not going to be convenient to get up early. I am not willing to stay home every day during the growing season either. So unless I have someone else to take over watering for me, I have to come up with some other way to make sure my garden gets watered.

Personally, I connect a water timer to my outside garden watering system. I program it to go on and off at specific times and then my watering gets done no matter where I am or what I have to do.

I can take a vacation, go fishing, or go to the beach and the garden gets watered anyway. I can sleep late and still get the garden watered early.

My suggestion is to purchase an outdoor timer that goes on your outdoor faucet. Then attach your hose to the timer and set it for the time you wish to start watering and for how long. Then turn it on and forget about watering until the end of the season. The only time you might want to change things is if your garden gets a lot of rain and extra watering is not needed or advisable.

Always be aware that more damage is done by not watering than is done by excess watering a few times a year. The timers are not expensive and I have seen them for roughly $20 or less. You can get a basic single time model or an advanced one with multiple times. It's your choice.

For those of your with lawn sprinkler systems you might be able to add a zone for your garden and control it with your lawn sprinkler timer. While this will work just fine, it should be mentioned that sometimes your garden will need to be watered less, or more often, than your lawn. When you use the same system for both purposes, something might get hurt in the process. The timers are so cheap and easy to use I believe it makes sense to use a separate and dedicated timer for your garden.

At the end of this book we will show you how to build a watering system to hook up to the timer to automate the watering of your entire garden! Gardening should be fun and not a chore. Automating the repetitive tasks is one way of keeping it fun without interfering with the rest of your lifestyle.

# Watering Methods

There are several ways to water your garden. Though the most important thing is getting enough water to properly nourish your plants, how that water gets to the plants might make a big difference in your garden as well!

## Hose Watering

This is a common method of watering a garden but also the most labor intensive and least accurate. While many people find standing at their garden and watering it to be a relaxing and calming experience, it is a time consuming and inaccurate way to watering.

It is inaccurate because you are manually moving the hose across parts of your garden in a random or inexact method. It does not guarantee that each of your plants gets the same amount of water nor does it guarantee that all plants receive any water!

The only advantage to this method of watering is that you can easily give more water to certain plants whenever you want.

## Root Watering

Root watering uses a hose or tubing that releases water directly into the soil without shooting it through the air. Hoses commonly called "soaker hoses" have a lot of holes in them that water leeches through and goes directly into the soil.

One of the advantages of this type of watering is that 100% of the water goes into the soil and very little is lost to evaporation. Another advantage is that you can more closely control exactly WHERE the water goes.

For example, you can run a loop of hose around each plant directly over the roots so the water just goes in that area. If you have plants that are spread apart very widely, this might help you make better use of your water.

But there are a few disadvantages of root watering as well. First, you cannot see the water actually going in the soil so if a hose gets clogged over time, which they are known to do, a plant might not get enough water and could die.

The exact opposite might happen as well if the holes should get bigger or the hose split and too much water gets into the soil turning it to mud and fostering mold and mildew and rot.

For me personally, I like to see the water going and hitting the plants. This makes it easy to spot a logged sprinkler, a broken hose, etc.

Another reason to use other methods is that plants absorb water from all over not just through their roots. So by watering from above and hitting the leaves and branches of plants, you can get water into the plant easier and faster. Plus, water has a cooling effect and that could help in very hot climates as well.

## Sprinkler Watering

Watering by sprinkler is very common as it is easy and requires little time or work. You can even make it easier by hooking the sprinkler to a garden hose timer and setting it to go on and off by itself. This can be really handy while you are away on vacation! Watering by sprinkler also allows you to set more precise times as well.

Just make sure that your sprinkler is hitting all the areas it needs to. I suggest monitoring and setting it in place at the exact time you plan on having it operational.

This is because water pressure can vary during the day and the lower the pressure the less area your sprinkler will cover.

Another problem is that on hot days when more people are watering their lawns, pressure will often go down and some plants might not get hit by the sprinkler. For this reason, monitor it closely and make adjustments as required. Sometimes using more than one sprinkler to overlap coverage can make for more uniform watering.

**Custom Watering**

Okay, bear with me here because although this type of system will take you more time to build and set up, it will save you hours and hours and hours of time and work for years to come. I have built one and it has lasted 5 years now and is still going strong.

What I did was design a watering system that covered all areas of the garden. I used sprinkler head available at any home center to cover all parts of the garden. The heads are cheap and the piping I used was old sprinkler tubing but you can use PVV and fittings as well. Cost is not high but it takes some time.

If you do decide to go this route, make sure you overlap the coverage on the heads. The head will have a diameter on it and I usually mount the heads so they overlap by roughly 50 percent.

Keep in mind that the more heads you put in the line the smaller the coverage area will be so it might take some trial and error to get things the way you want them. But after that it is hands free watering.

Just attach an exterior water timer and you are good to go whether you are home or not! This is definitely the best way to water! More details in the bonus section at the end of this book!

# Fertilizing

OK, here is where we really get into some simple things we all can do to increase our yield, grow bigger and healthier plants, and keep disease and insect infestation to a minimum. There are a few different ways to fertilize our plants. These range from natural substances to chemicals we can purchase in our local garden retailer.

First of all, let me say that whatever approach you decide to take, that is your preference and your right. There are folks who swear they will never put any chemical on their plants no matter what the reason and there are others who swear by certain chemicals. Neither is definitely right nor wrong in this regard. You should do whatever feels right and works for you. But you should also be open minded about the other methods should you ever find yourself in a situation where those methods might help you. Do not be close minded when it comes to anything!

Let's talk about chemical fertilizers and chemicals for a moment. I definitely believe there is a place in any garden for a good chemical fertilizer if the gardener is not averse to using it. I do recommend, however, that unless you have specific training and knowledge of these products that you stick with the general purpose over the counter fertilizers that you can find just about anywhere. Products like Miracle-Gro come to mind as being an accepted safe and well performing product. If you require a license to purchase or apply something, forget those products unless you can hire a professional to use them.

Whenever handling fertilizers or any garden chemical, wear gloves and a respirator if you are spraying or atomizing the chemical. While these products are safe, it is never a good idea to breathe in chemicals of any kind. It is better to be safe than sorry. Also, when you are done wash hands and arm thoroughly before eating or doing other activities.

Any product, no matter how well known and how safe, will only be that way if you apply it and mix it according to the directions on the box or bottle. There should be no situation where you should apply a higher concentration of any product. There might be times when you might want to mix it a little weaker than normal, like fertilizing seedlings or planting holes, but NEVER mix or apply it at a higher concentration than recommended.

Chemical fertilizers are measured by three numbers. On the bag you should see something like 5-10-5 or 20-10-10 or similar numbers. These numbers refer to the chemical composition of the product. The first number is the amount of nitrogen, the second number is the amount of potash and the third number is the amount of phosphate.

These numbers are important because different solutions will have different effects on our soil PH and other attributes. You should always know what your plants and soil need before purchasing and applying a fertilizer.

Some soils are rich in mineral and nutrients already and might only need a little "boost" while other soil might be almost totally deficient in everything and need a large amount of help in order to properly grow plants. Always use the proper fertilizer to bring your soil PH up to where your plants require. It is also a good idea to retest the level of PH in your soil a week or so after applying any kind of fertilizer since the chemical can cause the PH of the soil to change.

Never apply too much fertilizer to a plant as you run the risk of burning. For that reason, I always use a liquid fertilizer and a sprayer.

This is personal preference because my experience with powdered fertilizers can burn plants if applied too heavy. Once you spill powdered fertilizer on a portion of soil it is a LOT of work to remove it. I feel safer and more confident with liquid fertilizer.

While I do not use a lot of actual fertilizer on my garden, I will usually apply some liquid fertilizer a few days after my initial planting. This gives a little boost to the plants and helps them develop stronger roots. Also, at the beginning of the season mulch is not too high and a little liquid fertilizer will keep nutrients high enough until I can mulch.

For seeds and seedlings, there is a fertilizer called "compost tea" that is designed for seeds and young plants. It will not burn roots or harm plants when used and applied according to directions. There are also commercially available fertilizers meant for seed beds as well. Whichever fertilizer you might use for your plantings, just make sure it is mixed and applied as directed. Too high a concentrate can damage plants.

Apply fertilizer at the recommended intervals. Do not apply every other day. Too much fertilizer on tomatoes will results in really good looking plants with a LOT of leaves but too much of the plant energy is spent on producing leaves, not fruit. You don't want a lot of leaves and no fruit!

### Fertilizer Spikes

Fertilizer spikes for tomato plants contain a slow release fertilizer that is in the form of a spike that is hammered into the ground a certain distance from the plant. Hammer it into the ground the specified distance away from the plant. Do NOT place it closer or the plant can get burned. If the soil is hard and if any of the spike should break off or crumble during insertion, remove those pieces from the soil or they can burn the plants.

### Specialty Fertilizers

There are tons of specialty fertilizers out there for most plants and tomatoes are no exception. Feel free to try any of these and gauge for yourself which ones will work in your particular soil and region. As with many aspects of gardening, trial by error and personal preference are the keys to deciding which the best choice is for you. Gardening magazine will also have reviews of the latest products for your tomatoes as well. Knowledge is power so read up and get some experience!

## Fertilizer Tips

### Remember the Gap!

Whenever you apply any kind of powdered or granular fertilizer, keep it well away from the plant itself. This is because watering or rain may wash the fertilizer into the plant and cause a high concentration at the plant roots burning the plant. Always leave adequate space between fertilizer and plant stem. The dirt around the stem should be higher as well so fertilizer is not drawn to the plant but instead away from it.

**Water, Water, Water!**

Whenever you apply fertilizer it is important that you water the plant to reduce any inadvertent concentrations of fertilizer that can burn or harm the plant. Watering also helps wash fertilizer off leaves and other plant surfaces where it can burn as well.

**Wait for Fruit**

Fertilize your plants during planting but wait until the plant flower for the next application. After fruit is set you can fertilize again. Always follow the manufacturer's directions for applying fertilizer.

**Know Your Soil!**

Never apply any fertilizer until you know what the PH of your soil is. Then you can pick the right fertilizer for your plants. If you soil is correctly balanced or higher in nitrogen, try a 5-10-5 or a 5-10-5 fertilizer. If you soil is lacking in nitrogen, you can try an 8-8-8 or a 10-10-10.

## Mulching

The method I use for almost all my fertilizing needs is mulching. While we will have a complete chapter on mulch a little later on let me give you some information now on how mulch can save you time and energy and minimize the need or use of chemicals.

Mulch is a layer of organic material that is placed on top of the soil. Do not confuse mulch with the plastic or woven "weed blocker" material that sometimes has mulch in the name. That fabric adds nothing to the soil. Organic mulch, on the other hand, feeds the soil and produces very beneficial growing conditions for the plants. Mulch does this through a process referred to as decomposition.

As mulch decomposes, it releases nutrients into the soil. So think about mulching like a hospital IV dispenses medication. Mulch slowly releases food to the plants over long period of time.

It does so slowly and constantly just like the IV in your arm administers medication slowly and continuously into your arm.

Mulch also keeps the soil warmer which is good for the plants and can even prolong the gardening season. This heat also discourages weed seeds from germinating as well. So not only does mulch help your plants, it keeps weeds in check as well. Since weeds draw nutrients out of the soil, there is more food left in the soil for our plants. More food equals larger plants and larger harvests! Mulch also helps keep the nutrient level in the soil constant. Unlike piqued fertilizers that remain in the soil until they are absorbed or filtered out, mulch continues to feed the soil and heat the soil 24/7.

Mulching will eliminate, or at least significantly reduce, the need for most chemical fertilizers. Just be careful what you put in your mulch. If you spray chemicals on or near your mulch pile, those chemical will be in your mulch. The same with diseases and insects. Keep your mulch pile clean and well tended and you will have a never ending source of food for your plants.

More on mulching in our chapter on mulching!

# Weed Control

All gardeners hate weeds. We hate them because they look ugly and they represent work for us in removing them constantly over the course of the season. But our plants hate them as well for entirely different reasons. Weeds still nutrients from the soil and their roots sometimes prevent plant roots from growing as well. So weeds are bad and we need to get rid of them.

Here are some tips and techniques for minimizing weeds or possibly eliminating them entirely:

**Beware of Weed Killers**

First and foremost, remember that weeds are also plants like our vegetable plants in our garden. What we spray on weeds to kill them may also kill our plants as well. Weed killers like round-up and other brands will kill anything they come across and that means tomatoes, beans, cucumbers and everything else that is near the weeds.

For that reason, we recommend manual weed removal instead of chemical control.

Pre-emergent weed killer stop weed seeds from germinating and they will do the same for any seeds we plant to grow vegetable plants as well. Since pre-emergent chemicals are usually used early in the season, stay away from them if you are planting anything from seed.

**Start out Weed Free!**

Remove any weed you see while you are either building your garden bed from scratch or turning over the soil to start a new year! Removing weeds now will make for fewer weeds later since no new weed seeds will be deposited into the soil from existing weeds.

**Get the Whole Plant**

Weeds, like our other plants, have two parts. The first is what is above ground and that you can see. The second part is the root system that lies in the soil. If you just remove the top portion, the plant will simply grow new leaves and reappear. In order to get control of weeds you need to pull out the entire plant not just the top.

Sometimes a weed removal tool, short of like a narrow shovel, will help you dig down deeper into the soil and loosen the roots so you get the entire plant. If you leave even one root behind, the plant could quickly reappear.

**Make the Environment Bad for Weeds**

Weeds like good growing conditions just like our plant do. So we need to create lousy growing conditions for our weeds while at the same time creating better growing conditions for our plants. This is actually quite easy to do.

Mulch, the organic matter added to the top of our soil, can help destroy weed seeds before they turn into plant. The heat built up during decomposition can help prevent germination of weed seeds. In addition weeds that do germinate will have their roots in the loose mulch which make them very easy to pick up and pull out the entire plant.

Several inches of mulch will eventually wipe out most weeds and allow you to control weeds in just a few minutes of work every week. Mulch is the magic potion for feeding plants and controlling weeds.

**Don't Let Weeds Get Bigger!**

Don't let weeds sit and grow in your garden. Not only do they take nourishment and water from the soil, they will develop stronger and deeper roots systems over time making them much more difficult to remove and control.

Don't weed once a week, weed whenever you see a weed in the garden. Catching them while they are young and small will enable you to remove them before they get established and drop seeds into the soil causing more weeds!

**Keep Weeds out of Mulch!**

Mulch is great but only when the mulch is weed free. Do not place weeds in your mulch pile unless the heat generated during decomposition is hot enough to kill the plant and the seeds. I just take weeds away and keep them out of the pile. Remember anything you add to the mulch can also grow in the mulch.

**Spot Treat Severe Infestations**

If you have a particularly severe weed problem in some spots, consider a spot treatment that comes in a small spray bottle.

Instead of a large spray area from a garden sprayer you have a smaller spray that you can target on difficult areas without affecting other plants. If you go this route, try and apply the spot treatment on calm days as winds will take some of the material and spread it around surrounding plants.

**Weed control Fabric**

This material blocks sunlight from the soil and therefore prohibits weed growth. Some people use plastic sheeting for this purpose but that is not advisable for gardens because plastic does not allow water to go through either. The result is the water rushes into the holes for the plants and gets concentrated around the stem of the plant causing rot and uneven moisture in the soil.

Plastic also blocks sunlight from the soil which means no nutrients are added to the soil as well. Once the oil is depleted the plant will get stressed for food and possibly die. At the very least you will have some serious soil issues that will need to be addressed at the end of the season or next year.

Weed control fabric on the other hand will block out sun but allow moisture to pass through. It will still block certain nutrients from the soil as sunlight is still blocked.

The garden will have a nice and neat appearance, and weeds will not be an issue, but the surface is less than optimal when it comes to soil nutrients.

You also need to apply the bulk of any fertilizer before the fabric or plastic goes down as the larger granules of the fertilizer might not pass through. Also, the fertilizer might tend to wash along the surface and enter through the holes for the plants causing problems again.

Another reason I do not like to use cloth, and especially plastic, is that fungus and other organisms have a fairly sheltered area to form and grow. Dark and moist places are great areas for fungus to start and grow and I like to minimize that in the garden not encourage it. That is just my personal opinion on that though.

## Cultivation

Hey, if you like gardening work and weeding, why not give cultivation a try? I don't care for it because it is a weekly process that you must do regularly in order for it to be effective. Hand cultivating the soil helps dislodging growing weeds and interrupts their root growth. Using a sharp cultivator you are continually breaking up and destroying the roots of the plant.

I have to stress that this is not a one-time action that you take. You have to do it over and over and over throughout the entire gardening season. It is labor intensive but it does not require the use of chemical or the fabric or plastic so that is a plus for most of us.

## Shade

Weeds, like any other plants, need sun and do not like shade. Some gardeners will plant their crops closer together so that the shade from the plant blocks the sun from the soil thus keeping weeds away. There are a few problems with this, however.

First, when plants are small, little shade is provided so weeds will grow during that time. You will have to remove those weeds and keep doing so until the plant matures and gets larger so it can provide the needed shade.

Second, the sun is constantly moving and therefore the shade will move as well. So keeping entire areas out of the sun for the entire day is difficult. Even a few hours of sun can allow weeds to sprout and take hold.

Third, and this is a big one: Plants like tomatoes need a lot of sun and air movement in which to feed and grow.

When you plant tomato plants too close together you restrict their ability to grow full root systems and you block air and sun from some areas of the plant. This results in a lower yield from the plants. So you don't have as many weeds but you also have fewer and smaller tomatoes. It's your choice.

You might notice I don't get into chemical weed prevention very much in this chapter. That's because a) I don't use it and 2) there are so many factors when it comes to using chemicals I do not want to give the wrong advice and have someone blame me because their plants all died because of chemicals.

If you do wish to go the chemical route then I suggest you check with your local garden center (not a discount store where no one knows anything about gardening or plants) and find the safest weed control product and get instructions on how to apply it and use it. As always, wear gloves and a respirator during the application and wash your tools and hands and exposed skin immediately after use.

Regardless of the method you may choose, it is vital that you remove as many weeds as possible from your soil at all times. Do not let weeds get out of hand and then try and remove them. By that time they will have dropped seeds and more weeds will pop up next week.

In the meantime, those weeds will be taking nourishment and moisture meant for your tomato plants. This can, and usually will, reduce your yield and plant growth. The best thing you can do for your garden it to keep it weed free as much of the time as possible. Whether that is by chemicals, mulch, mechanical removal or by casting a spell over the garden to rid it of weeds, I don't care.

Just get rid of them and keep them gone. And do it safely.

# Mulching

This is where I believe I make the most difference when it comes to the health, size and yield from my plants. Mulch makes my soil softer and easier to work with and also nutrient rich. It also holds water extremely well.

If I apply a liquid fertilizer more than twice in a year that is a lot because most of my plants keep the majority of their nutrients from mulch, not actual fertilizer. You can get mulch from several sources. The most common, and the method that I use is from grass clippings. I apply the clippings to my garden after mowing. By the end of the season I have 6 inches of this nutrient rich material over my soil!

I empty the clipping directly on my garden as I mow. I start by placing a ring or mulch around each plant. I leave a few inches between the mulch and the young plants so it does not harm the plant or prevent air from reaching the base of the plant. Naturally, you should not allow the mulch to cover the plant in any way.

Plants should always be above the mulch to receive sunlight. If plants are very small and young, just leave more space between the mulch and the plant.

As I continue to mow into the season I eventually will cover the entire garden with mulch. When the entire garden is covered I apply a second layer, then a third and fourth and so on. After I am done applying mulch for that day I will water lightly to get it damp.

I should mention that some people believe that applying green clippings right from the lawn will actually remove nitrogen from the soil. I have not found this and my soil PH do not reflect this in my garden. I just wanted to bring this to your attention in case you wanted to look into that a little more. The one great thing that mulch does is keep the soil warm and moist. If you have several layers of mulch on your soil and you stick your hands down into it, you will feel heat. Be careful because sometimes this heat will be significant. For this reason I do NOT recommend walking barefooted on a mulched garden and always wear gloves to protect your fingers and hands. Mulch that is several inches high can also get slippery if you try to make a quick pivot or turn while walking. Do NOT rest a ladder on a mulched surface either as it can slip and slide on the mulch.

The decomposition process will produce extremely nutrient rich materials that plants just love, especially tomato plants. Even more impressive, it produces this material naturally and it will not burn or hard the plants either. In over 20 years I have NEVER had a plant suffer from over fertilization from mulch!

## Mulch Precautions

While mulch is one of the best ways to feed and nourish plants, there are a few things you should know when it comes to producing and using mulch. Here are a few of the most important ones:

**Insects** – If the source of your mulch had an insect problem, do not use those materials in your garden mulch. That is because you will just be adding those insects into your garden where they will feast on your plants and fruit.

**Dead Plants** – You can add dead plants to your mulch pile but only if they died from natural causes such as frost, end of harvest, lack of water, etc. If they died of a disease or fungus, remove the plants and throw them away! Just like insects, adding these plants to your mulch will just reintroduce the disease and fungus to your other plants. Throw these plants away! If there is any doubt, throw it out!

## Kitchen Waste & Mulch

While kitchen scraps and other materials can make great mulch, I would not place them directly on the garden soil. I would add those to your mulch pile or compost bin and let them decompose in their rather than in your garden. Scraps and rinds attract animals and insects and this could be harmful. In a compost bin the heat generated usually will kill any disease or insects and render the problem harmless. Even though this is the case I would still refrain from putting anything into our mulch pile that has any kind of problem.

## Lawn Clippings

Lawn clippings work so well for me that this is the only kind of mulch I use. My lawn provides me with all the mulch I need all season long. As I have already said I apply the clippings on the soil directly and have never had any problems doing so. But if this concerns you, the second option is to pile the clipping in the corner until they turn brown and then apply them to the garden. If you do this, be sure to turn over the pile from time to time to hasten the process.

If sections of your lawn should have an insect problem, then throw the clippings from that part of the lawn into the trash. If you are concerned about chemicals and your garden, do not use any clippings from your garden for a few weeks after your lawn has been treated.

## Making Mulch

There are a few ways to make mulch for your garden. You can place organic materials in a pile at a remote location or you can purchase a home compost bin and place the materials in there. Include lawn clippings, dead plants, kitchen scraps, even human waste can be used if that doesn't bother you!

If you use a compost pile, you will have to mix up the pile every week or so to get fresh air into the pile to hasten the decomposition process. If you use a compost bin, some of those have a handle that allows you to rotate the barrel to automatically mix up the contents. No matter how you do it, you must add fresh air into the pile periodically to continue the process.

If you are placing grass clippings right on your garden soil, you do not have to worry about turning it over or adding air because every week you will be adding layer after layer and trapping air into the mulch. Also, since a pile is very high, air cannot get to the center. When the mulch is spread out only an inch or two at a time, air can get in naturally.

The thicker the mulch the better it is for your garden. Mulch helps you control weeds and any weeds that do grow will have roots in the mulch which makes them easy to pull. The heat developed within the mulch helps it kill weed seeds and sprouts which reduces the overall number of weeds.

## Purchasing Mulch

As with everything else today, in some areas garden centers and farmers will offer mulch for sale. You should buy from only a responsible source where you have a good idea that no diseased plants or chemicals would be added. Remember the more you put in the mulch the more mulch you make so some people might put everything into their mulch whether it should be used or not.

Mulch can be stored until you use it. Covering your mulch pile is a good idea to keep animal and insects out. But you should keep your pile damp or even wet to aid and hasten the decomposition process. Do not allow the pile to dry out completely as both moisture and air are need for decomposition.

## Applying Mulch

Assuming your mulch is insect and disease free you can apply it to your garden at any time.

Application is pretty much straight forward. Just place a uniform layer of mulch over the parts of the garden you wish to mulch. Avoid clumps and piles. Just a nice flat and uniform layer of mulch all over. I apply mulch to the entire garden to control weeds as well as feed the plants. Even the areas without plants will benefit by the mulch. Mulch also helps keep the soil soft and absorbent as well.

I always leave a gap between the mulch and the plant, especially with new plants. This is to make sure that moisture can reach the plant as well as keeping the mulch away from tender plants until they fully harden off after a few weeks outside.

After laying the mulch down, apply water to dampen the mulch and moisten the soil. Water regularly afterwards as you normally would. Keep in mind that you might need less water after you apply mulch. If you see standing water on top of the mulch after watering, you may have to reduce the amount of water needed.

To confirm that water is getting through and that you are watering enough, pick a few spots in the garden and dig down through the soil about 6-8 inches. If everything is damp, and there is no mud, you are good to go. If areas are dry, then increase your watering. If there is mud or very wet soil, cut your watering back.

## Next Year Feeding!

Here is another area where using mulch makes things better and easier. At the end of the season, do not remove the mulch. Remove your plants but leave the mulch intact. Then till the entire garden to mix in the mulch with the soil. This will enrich the soil and make it easier to till next year and you will have better soil than you did starting this year!

Every year plants take away nutrients from our soil. That is why some people rotate their crops. But if you use mulch and till it under at the end of the season, the soil has all winter to decompose the mulch and feed the soil to replenish what was lost!

This makes the soil richer and looser next year. Tilling or turning over the soil will be much easier as well as planting your new plants. The soil will get better and better each year as you add mulch and nutrients into the soil!

I even take things one step further and add a layer of chopped leaves to the garden to help protect the soil over the harsh winters. I do this very easily by going over my lawn with a mower with a bag attached. I let the bag fill up but I do not empty the bag. I continue going over the lawn and the chopped leaves stay on the grass.

I then empty the bag into a garbage can or bag and then I go over the lawn again picking up the chopped up leaves.

The mower chops them up even finer and I empty the bag when it gets full and dump them right on the garden. It doesn't take very long to do my leaves this way and I feed my soil at the same time. Plus, there are no lawn bags to purchase and put out for the garbage.

Though this sounds like work I find it faster and much easier than raking by hand. Do NOT place full leaves on your garden as they will blow all over the place and will not decompose very fast. Doing the double mowing makes the leaves very fine and almost like a powder. The next year at the beginning of the season I roto-till everything into the soil and the result is a rich and loose soil that the plants just love.

All without chemicals or very few chemicals depending on what you prefer.

In the interest of complete disclosure, I should say that mulch can smell a bit. The actual smell will depend on what is used in the mulch itself. Grass clippings have a kind of sweet smell that I kind of like. The wife? Not so much. But the smell is temporary and will be made less by watering.

I do not believe there is a better way to feed our plants, protect our soil and improve the quality of our soil year after year.

Many of the problems plaguing gardeners for years can be minimized or even eliminated by using mulch.

It also makes the garden more attractive as well. Weeds have a difficult time in mulch so your weeding time goes down and you have this nice and uniform looking base for your garden. Certain plants like cucumber, squash and tomatoes really thrive with mulch because it provides food, moisture and heat to the soil all of which the plants respond well to.

Personally, I find that using mulch makes gardening easier and better. I would not think of having a garden without mulch. It is not only environmentally responsible and sound, it is economical as well. I hope you will give mulch a try in your garden. I'm sure once you start you will never stop!

# Disease

### Blossom End Rot

If your tomatoes have a sunken grayish area on the tomato chances you are have blossom end rot. This is fairly common and can usually be controlled with frequent irrigation and using mulch to control soil moisture.

### Sun Scald

If plants get too much sun, or if the sun and air is very hot, usually during the mid summer months, your tomatoes may get yellowish or orange spots on the fruit. This is because the sun has baked part of the tomato. To keep this from happening, increase fertilizer or mulch to get more foliage which will shield the tomatoes from the sunlight.

If you are pruning or trimming the plants, do not remove any more leaves to increase the shading of the fruit.

### Leaf Spot

Sometimes you will see brown spots or patches on the leaves of the plant. Leaves may even turn yellowish in extreme cases. This is because there is either too much shade on the plants which allows moisture from watering to stay on the leaves too long or a fungus has attacked the plant.

You can combat this by planting your plants far enough apart that they receive a lot of air movement which will aid in drying the leaves. Also, the further the plants are separated from each other, the more difficult it will be for the fungus to spread.

## Blight

Blight is a type of fungus that causes the lower leaves of the plant to develop black spots or turn yellow and die. Fungicide can help control and eliminate blight in its early stages. Gray circular areas with a velvet like appearance are indications of blight on the fruit. Remove an infected fruit immediately. Warm and humid or damp conditions are good for causing blight.

## Anthracnose

Spotted fruit with the appearance of spores and the early death of plants is a common symptom of anthracnose.

This is a fungus that can be spread by leaving last year's plants on the ground or in mulch where the disease can thrive and spread. But it can also infect plants during the current growing season as well.

Fungicides might help and picking of all fruit right when they become ripe will help as well. This is one reason to remove and discard old plants instead of mulching them.

**Funguses and Rot**

There are several different types of fungus that live on or near tomato plants. Almost always it is because the condition on or around the plant are either very humid and moist or shady or a combination of both.

The best way to control fungus is to not let it get started in the first place. Do not water late in the evening or overnight. Water early in the morning so the sun can burn off the top of the soil or mulch and the plant leaves.

Plant properly so that there is a lot of air movement which will also aid in drying plus reduce the dampness as well. Inspect regularly and if you see signs of mold of fungus on the soil or the mulch slowly and carefully remove it. Do so slowly so you do not cause any of it to become airborne in the process.

Early detection is the key so that we can get a handle on the problem before it becomes too invasive. Mold can grow very quickly in the right environment. So what we need to do is make sure we provide as unfriendly as possible place for fungus to grow.

These are just a few of the common diseases and fungus problems you can experience on your plants. Some other diseases or conditions can cause similar symptoms yet be different problems. The best way to determine exactly what you have is to bring a sample of the damaged fruit or plant to your local garden center or agriculture office and have them look at it.

If these offices or places are not local, perhaps you can take a clear and sharp digital picture and e-mail it to people who can advise you. As always, the quicker you notice the problem and correctly identify it, the faster you will be able to properly treat the problem and minimize damage.

Whenever a plant is either removed or infected parts removed, discard those parts into the trash and do not mulch them. The disease is likely to thrive in the mulch and come back with a vengeance once the mulch is added to your soil.

**Preventive Care**

Some gardeners believe strongly that take a pro-active approach to garden problems is the best way to go. As far as diseases and fungus are concerned, we can apply commercial fungicides and use insecticides as well for other problems.

While this means inserting chemicals into your garden, there may be little else you can do after you have exhausted correcting the environmental we have discussed in this book. Sometimes the region in which we live has its own set of organisms that can cause you problems no matter what you do.

I would check with your local garden center at the beginning of the year and let them inform you of any known problems or issues that have been reported in the area. Once you are aware of them you can decide if you want to proactively treat your garden to help minimize or prevent any damage.

There are arguments both for and against doing this but only you can decide which approach you are comfortable with. Be aware that sometimes by the time you see damage it might be too late to save your plants. In those cases preemptive treatment might be the only way to save your garden.

Experience plays an important role as well. If you have had problems in the past, it is likely they will surface again because they are in your area.

So if you lose some plants to a fungus this year, you might want to apply a fungicide at the end of the season and next season as well to kill off any remaining fungus and prevent new fungus from coming back.

As with any chemicals, apply as directed and wash your hands and wear a respirator during application. Clean all tools and the sprayer when you are finished.

# Insect Control

As if weeds weren't enough of a pain, nature has also given us insects to deal with in our garden. To be fair, insects play a very important role in nature and we need them to keep other species in check as well as for cross pollination of our plants.

We need and want to see bees hopping from flower to flower as this is how out plants produce fruit. Without pollination, there would be little for us to east in the way of vegetables. Larger insects are like the praying mantis, are good for our gardens as well because they eat the small and more dangerous insects that eat our plants. So let's just agree that some insects are good and beneficial for our garden.

But there are some insects that are bad for our plants and some that particularly enjoy munching on our tomato plants and their fruit. Those insects are what we will concentrate on in this chapter.

The most deadly insect is the **cutworm**. These bugs can be an inch to 2 or 3 inches long and about the size of a pencil or your finger. They are green so they blend in nicely with the plant itself. That is what makes them difficult to find. A cutworm will strip the entire plant bare of branches and leaves if left unchecked. They can do this in a day or so and then they will move on to another plant.

If you should happen to see a branch stripped clean, look above or below for a cutworm. You will probably see one or two somewhere on the plant. When you do, pick it off the plant, then squash it, whack it, or run it over with your car or motorcycle. Just do whatever you have to in order to render it lifeless!

Then, when the bug has ceased to be, continue looking up and down the tomato plant, and other tomato plants in your garden for other cutworms. They often travel in groups. I am sure somewhere there are little miniature motorcycles that these troublemakers ride to your garden on. (No offense to the bikers reading this! It's all in fun! I own a bike as well!) In any case, the good thing about cutworms is that they are easy to spot once you start looking for them.

**Aphids** are another thing all together. They will damage the leaves and plant structure. They are small and can be black, gray or green or yellow. They excrete a sweet chemical that can quickly turn into mold which will do further damage to the leaves and plants. If you notice aphids, you can wash them off with a strong spray of water. Then use an insecticidal soap to kill off those that are remaining and to eradicate the infestation. This will allow the plant time to stat healing. One sign of aphids is yellowing of the leaves.

Holes in the fruit itself can come from **tomato worms** or **small slugs**. If you see holes in the fruit, remove the infected fruit and discard. Use insecticidal soap to eradicate those remaining.

## Prevention

The only way to prevent infestation is to make the environment something the insects do not like. You can use a broad spectrum insecticide like Sevin which has been proven safe and has been around for decades. Just take care and mix and apply according to the directions. Make sure you use gloves and a respirator while applying the Sevin. Wash all sprayers and tools and hands immediately after application.

You can also use natural methods to control pests. If you have a specific insect problem, check to see if there are other insects that feed on those insects and bring them into your environment. Or make the garden itself unfriendly to the insects.

For example, if you have a problem with slugs, place charcoal embers around the garden or rough rocks or gravel. Slugs hate crawling over sharp objects and will not enter your garden if they have to travel over them.

The best form of prevention is awareness. Inspect your garden regularly for signs of insect damage. Address each problem quickly and thoroughly. Do the job right the first time. Getting rid of half the insects is not going to work. Some insects reproduce very quickly and the problem will continue to grow and grow until you intervene.

Get rid of conditions that insects like. For example, standing water attract mosquitoes. Eliminating the standing water makes the mosquitoes look elsewhere. Wash plants regularly or whenever you see indications of insect presence on the plants. Hand pick off any insects you see on the plants. If you see insects figure there are others that you cannot see as well. Apply an insecticidal soap to eradicate the infestation.

Some gardeners like to use an insecticide as a preventative as well. There are always insects in your garden. The problem, or concern, with using insecticides indiscriminately is that many of these insecticides do not selectively kill just the bad insects. They kill most of the insects both good and bad. This is not good as far as balance in nature is concerned.

So we need to balance out the pros and cons of using insecticides. Some gardeners use insecticides proactively while others wait to notice a problem and then use insecticides as treatment. The problem is that sometimes by the time you notice an infestation it might be too late to avoid considerable plant damage.

There is no single right approach. Everyone is different and everyone's garden is different as well. The only thing I can say is that you need to act responsible when using any chemical. That goes especially for insecticides. Be especially careful when there are babies or small children around. Keep all chemicals on the highest shelves or in secured and locked cabinets.

Insecticides are designed to kill insects so we need to understand that there are at least some dangerous chemicals involved. These products are designed to kill whereas fertilizers are designed to make things grow. That alone should indicate that they should be treated with a certain degree of respect.

It is not my intention to frighten anyone or scare them into refusing to use these chemicals. They have valid uses and have been proven safe when used according to directions. What my intention is, however, is to make sure we handle these chemical carefully and safely at all times.

## A Word Regarding Using Insecticides

While there are several ways to avoid using fertilizers and still adequately feed your plants, insect problems are a little more difficult to control without using insecticides. Insects rarely come alone. They usually bring friends so manual removal will just reduce, but not eliminate, the problem.

Insecticides like soaps and Sevin have been around for a long, long time and many studies have been made to test their effectiveness and overall safety. The chemicals are safe as long as used according to the instructions. Often time's insect infestation will require the use of one of these chemicals in order to resolve the problem.

Even physical removal of an entire plant might not work. Insects can fall off or fly off of plants as they are removed and go to other plants. Insects often reproduce quickly and one or two insects today could turn into several hundred next week or next month.

Some insects are able to become airborne and travel quickly and easily from one plant to another. This makes them even more difficult to remove. Do what needs to be done and use insecticides and soaps when called for. Otherwise your insect problem could take over your entire garden.

# Staking or Caging

While tomatoes can be grown along the ground, I find that this not only makes it difficult to walk around in the garden but also makes it easier for fruit to encounter disease and insect damage as well. There is a debate on whether it is better to stake or cage plants instead of letting them grow on the ground. The following is my personal preference based on the reasons that I will provide. In other words, this works for me and it should work for you. It is up to you to decide on which approach is right for you. Staking or caging does take more time and more work, but I believe it is worth it.

I initially use tomato cages to support and control the growth of my seedlings. When my plants reach the top of my cages, usually by the middle of summer or so, I then insert stakes to control the rest of the growth. So I guess you can say that I used a combination of both methods.

If your plants stay to about 3-4 feet then cages alone may be satisfactory. Cages are easier as you just have to feed the branches through the holes in the cages as the plants grow. There is no tying or anything else required. The cages provide all the support your plants will need at that size.

But if you follow my program for growing tomatoes, you are likely to find that your cages will quickly become too short as your plants may eventually grow 2-3 feet higher than their cages! In that case, I insert a wooden stake roughly 8 feet tall, into the ground away from the base of the plant. I hammer in the stake at least a foot into the ground while standing on a ladder or step stool to get above the stake.

I find that 1 X 2 pieces of wood are both adequate and inexpensive. Though not treated for outdoor use, I get 2 or 3 seasons out of one stake and they cost less than $2 each. I did have one year where my plants grew so large and the fruit was so heavy that they broke the 1 X 2 stakes, though. Since that time I have taken great care to make sure the plant grows around the stake and that there is not a lot more plant weight on one side of the stake. Balancing the plant around the stake in this manner will greatly increase the weight the stake will be able to carry.

I attach the branches to the stakes with rolls of garden ties. Garden ties are pieces of wire with a plastic coating over the wire so that it will not cut through the skin of the branch or stem of the plant. I buy my garden ties at a local flea market where they are cheap. You can usually find them at 99 cent stores and discount houses as well.

I support the branches with ties long before the branches fall over from weight. Once the branch falls over it can break and will have to be removed. With a little bit of experience you can see quite easily when support is needed. Every foot or so is a good starting point for when to tie off the branches.

When using the ties first wrap around the tie twice on the stake. This will increase the weight holding capacity of the tie. Twist the end around the tie several times to secure it. Then move the branch to where you want it and wrap it very loosely twice around the branch and secure in the same manner. You want to wrap it very loosely so the branch can grow thicker as it needs to. A good place to put the tie is right below a leaf or smaller branch is attached to the main branch. The other branch provides a barrier from the tie sliding down the branch.

As the season goes on you will have a lot of ties around the stake. This can be a time consuming process depending on how many plants you have in your garden.

But do not neglect it and let the branches get too long without support. It is much easier to do it a few times a week when the branches are not that long. Just like weeding, constant attention is better in the long run.

## Why Cage or Stake at All???

Here's where the debate comes in. Personally, I found more damage and less fruit with tomatoes allowed to grow along the ground. I also found more rotting of the fruit and more insect damage. For me, the answer was obvious.

The fruit and the plants lie right on the damp mulch and this can help disease and fungus grow on the plant. In addition, ground crawling insects can crawl right up to the food and eat away to their hearts content. It is so much more difficult to spot insect damage on plants lying on the ground. By the time you might spot the damage it could be too late.

I strongly believe that my harvests are larger because the plants are allowed to get more sunlight and air movement because they are staked and caged. The garden is a lot neater and travel through the garden is vastly easier and you can walk without hearing that sickening sound of you stepping on a nice 2 pound beefsteak hidden under some plant leaves.

We will talk about trimming of our plants next and having them in cages or on stakes make the trimming process go vastly easier and faster as well. Our focus should be on what is best for our plants and for ourselves as well. Cages and stakes do require some work but they also make other tasks easier as well.

Mulching, for example, cannot be easily or effectively done when pants are laying on the soil. The mulch will cover and possibly burn the plant unless we physically lift or move the plant while we are applying the mulch. Moving a plant greatly increases the chance of damage or breakage as well. When plants are in cages applying more mulch is quick and easy. We all know when something is quick and easy we are far more likely to keep on doing it.

That means we will continue to apply mulch and continue to inspect and maintain our plants. I strongly believe that my cages and stakes have a very positive effect on how my plants thrive and one of the main reasons they produce high yields year after year. This is really not rocket science. It is just a huge helping of common sense.

# Trimming Your Plants

All the energy and nutrients needed by your tomato plants must come from either through the leaves for sunlight or through the roots for minerals and moisture. The roots have a limit on how much they can transport at any given time and the plant itself has limits on what they can deliver to each branch and tomato.

Because of this, some gardeners like to trim their plants to remove excess leaves and branches. The idea is to direct more of the energy to producing more fruit and larger fruit. This is a labor intensive process and you have to make sure that you do not remove too many leaves or branches. The sun uses leaves to capture sunlight to feed the plant. If there are no leaves, the plant can die. It's simple as that.

One easy method of removing excess foliage is to remove the leaves that sometimes grow at the joint where branches meet the stem of the plant.

Gardeners sometimes refer to these leaves as "suckers" because they suck moisture and minerals from the plant. These leaves start off very small but will grow over time. You can snap off these sucker leaves or cut them off with a pair of garden snips.

Take great care no to nick or cut the branches or stem of the plant while removing these leaves. This can damage the plant and any opening in the skin of the plant is a potential opportunity for disease and fungus to enter the plant and create damage.

You should also remove any leaves that start to turn yellow. This will usually happen to the lower leaves as the plants grow taller and mature. The original leaves turn yellow and wilt. Remove those leaves to remove them from accepting food from the plant.

Another school of thought is to remove the lower branches of the plant after the plant has grown and become established. The very low branches generally will not have any flowers or fruit on them and probably are in the shadows of the plant and do not receive any sun either. Removing these branches will also help the plant concentrate on delivering more food and energy to the fruit and not to areas of the plant that are not needed.

Naturally, and areas of the plants that show signs of disease or stress should be removed as well.

Yellowing of leaves, insect damage, fungus and other problem areas should be removed from the plant so that these issues do not spread to the rest of the plant. In these cases you should remove any damaged areas to avoid spreading. If the damage is too severe and too many leaves have been removed, the plant may not survive. But at least you have saved your other plants in the garden from the same fate.

I know some of you might be tired of hearing this but trimming of your plants is largely a personal preference. I do not do a lot of trimming because I sometimes grow 20 plants and do not have the time to do the job right. Would my tomatoes be even larger or more plentiful? My guess is probably that they would. But I am not entering the world's largest tomato contest and my harvest and yield is already more than I need. So I spend my time doing other things that I get more reward or benefit from.

But if you grow just a few plants, or if you want to get the absolute largest fruit or the most fruit from your plants, you might wish to consider pruning or trimming your plants. If you unsure of the benefit, why not pick one plant and trim it and compare harvests to see if it was worth the effort. At the risk of repeating myself yet again, gardening involves a lot of personal preference and there is no right and wrong when it comes to trimming or not trimming your plants.

# End of Season

While every good thing must come to an end, you can do things to get the most from your garden this year and next with some very simple end of season procedures. Doing these simple things will enable you to get more fruit near the end and also prepare your garden for next year.

Frost is a killer when it comes to fruit and plants. When frost hits the internal structure of the plant freezes and expands. This destroys the tissue of the plant as well as the fruit. So after a frost our plants will die and any fruit on them will be destroyed.

We may be able to delay this a little bit by using mulch to protect the plant but this will not save you much since the majority of the damage occurs above ground. But we can do things to the plant to get them to divert more energy to the fruit to get them to ripen faster. We can cut off the tops of the plants where no fruit is growing as well as lower branches where fruit has already been harvested.

If you have been trimming or pruning your plants throughout the season then some of this work has already been completed thus making the job easier. But if there are branches not carrying fruit that can be removed, remove them now. If there is growth above where the fruit is growing, cut those back as well. The idea is to get as much food and energy into the fruit as possible.

If, despite your efforts, there are still fruit on the plant and you know a frost is going to hit, you can remove those tomatoes that you feel have started to ripen and place them in a box full of newspapers. Close the box and store it someplace for a week or so. Open the box from time to time and remove any fruit that has started to ripen. Fruit that is close to ripe can be removed and stored on a sunny shelf or ledge inside to complete the ripening process.

After the frost, dead or dying plants must be removed. Personally I do not mulch my old plants because the branches and stalks take a long time to decompose and there is always the possibility that they have insects or disease on them and placing them in my mulch pile could give these issues an environment for growth during the winter. Plus, the remaining fruit will have seeds inside and if you put those in your mulch pile, you will have little tomato plants popping up all over the place when it gets warmer next year! In fact, fruit that has fallen during the year has produced some nice plants for me the next year!

Take your plants and place them in large plastic leaf bags and toss them out with the garbage. This will help protect the rest of your garden as well. Again, this is personal preference and if you wish to mulch your old plants, and you inspect them for disease and insects first, then by all means go ahead and do so.

After your plants have been removed, now is the time to start preparing for next season and to take easy steps now that will make starting your garden next year even easier. In fact, some of the things you do now will have a huge effect on your next year's growth and harvest. That is why many gardens that follow my plan do even better in their second and third years! A little time spent now will pay huge dividends later!

## Till your soil

The very best thing you can do for your garden next season is to help prepare the soil this season. Roto-till the top mulch into the soil where it will help keep it loose and aid decomposition. This will produce a very rich and well-draining soil that will feed the plants next year from the minute they are planted.

Do two passes if you are using a powered tiller. One pass up and down followed by a second pass right to left. I have a large garden and two passes takes me less than 20-30 minutes. There is no need to be really careful like there is when preparing a bed for planting. We just want to get everything mixed down in the soil where it can decompose and help the soil recover during the winter.

Another reason to do this is to get air into the soil as well. Melting snow will slowly release moisture into the soil aiding decomposition even more. The result is a very loose and nutrient rich soil for next season.

**A Layer of Protection**

If you have leaves in your area, chop them up finely with your lawnmower and spread them across the top of the soil. This will not only help keep the soil warmer but will protect it as well. Next year, these leaf bits will be tilled down into the soil forming yet another layer of food and nourishment for the plants.

Doing this will keep the nourishment of the soil going all year round. What decomposed over the winter is not replenished with material that will be decomposing through the growing season.

Then the mulch added during the season will be tilled into the soil and the process continues. It is the very best and most economical way to produce excellent soil and free fertilizer for your plants. All without chemicals.

The other important thing this does is prevent wind from blowing away any of the really good soil you created over the last year or two. Our soil should be nice and loose and wind can blow this away. Having a nice protective layer of mulch over the soil will keep your soil exactly where it is. If some mulch blows away, that's not a big deal at all. Mulch can be easily replaced. Quality, nutrient rich, soil cannot.

Last, but certainly not least, the layer of mulch will prevent most of the airborne weed seeds from taking up residence in your garden. They will just sit on top of the mulch and their roots will find it difficult to establish themselves. If they do manage to take hold they will be easy to take out in the spring as they will be very shallow rooted. Pulling out the weed will easily removing the entire plant, roots and all.

## PH Balance

At the end of the season, check your soil PH and make any adjustments you need to make.

Adding lime, if needed, can be done now as well. It will hasten decomposition during the winter. The key is to keep the soil at the PH it needs to be year round so there are not massive changes required at any time. Winter time is no different.

If you wait until planting time and then find that you need to add massive amounts of anything to get your soil PH correct, then you run the risk of burning roots and plants. Take a few moments now to get your soil right so that only minor adjustments are needed come the spring.

## Tools

Our tools that we use should be given a little bit of TLC now as well. Rinse off your trowels and hand tools and give them a coat of automotive wax, or spray silicone spray on them to ward off rust. Sharpen you cutters and pruners so they make nice clean cuts and not ragged ones that can make it easier for disease to enter the plant.

If you are fortunate enough to own a roto-tiller, then clean that up as well. Remove dead plant matter that might have wrapped itself around the tines. If it is a 4 cycle machine then change the oil. It costs on a few dollars and takes just a few minutes but keeping fresh oil in the tiller. Just call it protecting your investment.

# 25 Tips for Creating the Best Tomato Plants!

1) Buy quality plants – do not skimp on cheaper or distressed plants.
2) Plant the right varieties for your area.
3) Prepare the soil properly before you plant.
4) Choose a location that provides the most light and moisture.
5) Get plants up off the ground in cages or use stakes.
6) Water properly and often.
7) Avoid plant stress whenever possible.
8) Trim or prune plants to remove dead leaves and "suckers".
9) Store picked fruit in a cool location approx. 60 degrees.
10) Test soil PH regularly and keep it at optimum levels.
11) Use mulch to feed plants and control moisture.
12) Inspect plants for insects and disease often
13) Till soil down to a depth of at least 6 to 8 inches or more.
14) Add mulch to the soil and till it under in the fall.
15) Pick fruit as soon as it ripens.
16) Use starter or seed fertilizer when plants are planted.
17) Move roots away from seedling so they get surrounded by the soil when planted

18) Remove weeds at least weekly from all areas of the garden
19) Allow plenty of air movement around all plants
20) Avoid creating an environment that is dark and moist to avoid fungus growth
21) Fertilize just after flowers appear on plants. Then again when fruit appears.
22) Create a mulch pile to produce nutrient rich soil for your garden
23) Protect and feed soil during the winter by tilling and covering in the fall.
24) Water more when it is very hot.
25) Enjoy gardening. Let someone else do the things you don't like to do!

# No Work Watering System!

OK! I'm going to show you something that is worth the price of this book and probably a lot more! I'm going to show you how to build an easy automatic watering system for your garden! It's easy, costs only a few dollars, and will give you perfect results every year!

I built my watering system and placed it on the top of a trellis that I grow my cucumbers on. But even if you don't use a trellis, you can easily build a support to hold your own watering system. I built mine out of wood but you can easily build it from PVC pipe. That would be more expensive but it would last longer than the wood will.

I use shrub sprinkler heads and black PVC sprinkler tubing to build my system. These parts and pieces are available at all home centers and are usually used in underground sprinkler systems.

Most garden systems can be built for about $20 plus the timer if you use one.

Although your system can vary, I place the heads about every 5-6 feet and have them sit about 5-6 feet high. Assembly is easy, just cut the black tubing to length, slip a screw clamp over the tubing and then push on a t fitting for the middle heads or an end fitting at either end, and tighten the clamp. Place a riser (threaded piece that goes in the fitting and you screw the sprinkler to on the other end) in each fitting and then screw a sprinkler nozzle on the riser. Assembly should take you less than an hour.

Here is a close up view of how each head is attached:

Notice you have one threaded piece which you screw the riser into and the sprinkler head that screws on the top. The end heads are the same except the fitting does not have two hose connections, just one.

I find that the 5-6 spacing works very well. There is some overlap which insures that everything gets watered even if water pressure should drop at times.

If you are building a trellis, make sure you use pressure treated wood so it will last for several seasons. My current system is over four years old and has required no maintenance.

## Connecting Your System

You can purchase a hose fitting that allows you to connect a garden hose to the sprinkler tubing. Then you can connect this to an outside faucet.

For a super easy automatic system, you have two options. You can purchase an outdoor garden timer and program it to come on whenever you want it. You can set the time, the day, and how long you want it to be on. Once you have figured out the best duration, you just set it and forget it. Your system will deliver the set amount of water every single day whether you are home of not!

The only time you might want to get involved with your watering is when you have several days of rain. In that case, you might want to shut the timer off until you need it so you don't waste water or over water.

Another option you might have is connecting it to your in ground lawn sprinklers.

If you have an unused spot on your timer, and you know how to add a zone onto your system, just add another zone valve and program it appropriately. If you don't know how to do this you can get your sprinkler company to add one for you.

I am a strong believer in automatic systems because it takes the "human element" out of the system. If you are busy at work, or tired or sick, or away on vacation, you may forget to water your garden or have to rely on others who may also forget. In either case, missing a few days of water in a hot time could cost you your entire garden.

Besides, gardens should be an enjoyable past time and not one filled with work and commitments. You can always shut your system off should you feel like a little manual watering. That is always an option. But it has always been my feeling that people stick with things that involve less work and less commitment. Plus, you plants do better with the right amount of moisture. The cost is minimal and the benefits are many. It really makes no sense to stand out in the yard every morning to water your garden. Let technology do it for you!

# FREE Gardening Information!

We would like to thank you for purchasing this book on growing tomatoes. To show our appreciation, we would like to send you a free report with some more information on gardening that will help you get better results from your tomatoes and other plants.

There is no obligation on your part to get this free report. Just click on the link below, or copy and paste it into your web browser to access the webpage. It's our way of saying thank you and helping you grow an even better and more impressive garden.

http://www.howtomastery.com/tomatoes.html

Made in United States
Orlando, FL
10 December 2023

40602668R00065